Survival Notes for New Parents

SURVIVAL NOTES FOR NEW PARENTS

INSPIRATION FOR AN
AMAZING ADVENTURE

BY
ROBERT STOFEL

Paulist Press
New York/Mahwah, NJ

Except where noted, scripture quotations are taken from the HOLY BIBLE, NEW INTERNATIONAL VERSION®. NIV®. Copyright ©1973, 1978, 1984 by International Bible Society. Used by permission of Zondervan. All rights reserved.

Scripture quotations marked (NLT) are taken from the HOLY BIBLE, NEW LIVING TRANSLATION, copyright © 1996. Used by permission of Tyndale House Publishers, Inc., Wheaton, Illinois 60189. All rights reserved.

Book and cover design by Jennifer Conlan

Copyright © 2008 Robert Stofel

All rights reserved. No part of this book may be reproduced or transmitted in any form or by any means, electronic or mechanical, including photocopying, recording, or by any information storage and retrieval system without permission in writing from the Publisher.

Library of Congress Cataloging-in-Publication Data

Stofel, Robert, 1962-
 Survival notes for new parents : inspiration for an amazing adventure / by Robert Stofel.
   p. cm.
 ISBN 978-0-8091-4590-4 (alk. paper)
 1. Parents--Religious life. I. Title.
 BV4529.S755 2008
 248.8'45--dc22
                                        2008038534

Published by Paulist Press
997 Macarthur Boulevard
Mahwah, New Jersey 07430

www.paulistpress.com

Printed and bound in the United States of America

*Dedicated with love and affection to Jill,
my loving wife and the wonderful mother of our children.*

Contents

Acknowledgments xi
Introduction 1
  1. Parenthood: There's No Owner's Manual 3
  2. The Language of Our Baby's Cry 5
  3. Parenthood: A Quick-Start Guide 7
  4. "Perfection" Is Not a Term in Parenthood .9
  5. Cooking like Martha Stewart While Smiling like Katie Couric . . .11
  6. Picking Up around the House Shouldn't Be a Lonely Job 13
  7. Why You Will Never Be a Terrible Parent 15
  8. Throw a Party for Older Siblings 17
  9. Building Trust with Your Baby 19
 10. What You'll Talk about When You Talk about Love 21
 11. Burning the Candle at Both Ends 23
 12. It's Your Turn to Change the Diaper! 25
 13. Why Every Parent Should Take a Power Nap 27
 14. Obsessing over Discipline 29
 15. How to Get the Funk Out 31
 16. Oh! The Questions They Will Ask 33
 17. Children Are a Gift from God 35
 18. Don't Be Afraid to Analyze Your Child .37
 19. The Mystery of Handicapped Children .39
 20. How Long, O Lord? 41
 21. Out of the Mouths of Babes 43
 22. Don't Forget about Yourself 45

23. How to Lose the Post-Pregnancy Weight 47
24. A Parent's Prayer 49
25. Teaching Our Children about God 51
26. A Parent's Frustration Level 53
27. How to Drive Selfishness from Your Child 55
28. Cutting Teeth and Gnawing on Toys 57
29. What to Do before You Sleep 59
30. Has Your Child Met the Mighty Milestones? 61
31. Safety First, Safety Last, Safety Always 63
32. The Days of Their Lives 65
33. How to Use Your Child's Middle Name 67
34. Where to Go for Advice 69
35. Modifying the Terms of Friendship 71
36. Setting Speed Limits for Your Child 73
37. Being Rich Is Not a Sin 75
38. Who Said You'd Become like Your Mother? 77
39. The Willingness to Succeed as a Parent 79
40. Parents Rule! 81
41. The Plans We Make May Not Be the Way They Choose 83
42. Quit Being so Serious 85
43. How to Mean What You Say and Say What You Mean 87
44. The Amazing Promise to Every Parent 89
45. To Breastfeed or Not to Breastfeed 91
46. Adventures in Babysitting 93
47. Should You Work or Stay at Home? 95
48. Bills! Bills! Bills! Dealing with the Money Crunch 97

49. How to Fall in Love Again 99
50. Feel Overwhelmed? 101
51. The Wrong Occupation for Every Mother 103
52. Shoot the Bull with Your Spouse 105
53. What a Father Should Never Do 107
54. Danger Never Takes a Vacation 109
55. Why Your Child Should Suffer the Consequences 111
56. Why a Baby Changes the Chemistry of Your Marriage 113
57. You Must Hate the Word "Must" 115
58. The Money Crunch 117
59. How a Father Can Make His Child Listen 119
60. Dealing with Separation Anxiety 121
61. Liar, Liar, Pants on Fire 123
62. Daily Face Time 125
63. Getting Daddy in the Game 127
64. The Power of Dr. Seuss's Words 129
65. Babies and Their Toys 131
66. How to Fix a Fussy Baby 133
67. Screaming Babies 135
68. Learning to Transition through Growth Stages 137
69. How to Pray for Our Children 139
70. Listen for the Whisper of God's Call 141
71. How to Calm an Angry Child 143
72. There Are No Homely Babies 145
73. Oh! The Places You Won't Go 147
74. State the Obvious for Problematic Relatives 149

75. Peek-a-Boo 151
76. Sweet Dreams 153
77. The Pain of Divorce 155
78. Stop That Whining! 157
79. How to Get Happy 159
80. Being Fair to Grandparents 161
81. Pets and Babies 163
82. From the Crib to the Bed 165
83. Reach Back Once You Get There 167
84. Remember the Romance 169
85. How to Get out of the Pits 171
86. What You Should Be Talking About 173
87. A Unified Front 175
88. Potty Time 177
89. Renew Your Commitment as a Parent Each Day ...179
90. Armchair Husbands 181
91. Friends Don't Let Friends Compete 183
92. Why You Should Pray with Your Spouse 185
93. How to Choose the Right Day Care 187
94. Teaching Your Child How to Make Friends 189
95. Picky Eaters 191
96. The Hidden Controller 193
97. Before and After Snapshots 195
98. Mothers Teach Their Children How to Treat Them ...197
99. We Can Love Them Too Much 199
100. The Winter of Our Parenthood 201
About the Author 202

ACKNOWLEDGMENTS

I thank Paulist Press for their vision and dedication. Jennifer Conlan enhanced this book with her heart, soul, and wisdom.

Thanks to my own father and mother who helped shape my parenting skills.

Thanks to my two daughters, Blair and Sloan, who taught me that parenting is 95 percent love and dedication.

Thanks to Vintage Faith, the people who know me and love me the most.

INTRODUCTION

Receiving the gift of children seems too wonderful and delicate for our unskilled hands. Parenthood can seem daunting when you are alone with your newborn for the first time. But God knew what he was doing when he fashioned your baby in the womb. He selected you to be the parent. He knew you'd be perfect—not perfect without flaws—but perfect because he knows you will do your best to raise your child in godly ways. Because if we train our children in God's ways, when they are old, they will not turn from it (Prov 22:6). As parents, the greatest thing we will do is train them in God's ways.

God will never leave you. He will lead and guide you through unknown territory. He will support you through the words in this book. He will send help in the form of wonderful family members or friends. God is there beside you. Comforting you. Watching over you. Believing in you. So don't worry about not knowing everything about parenting. No one begins the journey of parenthood with everything figured out. Nothing worthwhile comes to us overnight. Enjoy the journey. Do the best you can. Love like a parent. Love like a friend. Love will be your gift back to your newborn. And love will be enough, as love always is. You will be a great parent!

*A*dam lay with his wife Eve, and she became pregnant and gave birth to Cain. She said, "With the help of the LORD I have brought forth a man."

— *Genesis 4:1*

ONE

Parenthood: There's No Owner's Manual

The staff at the hospital will wish you well as they will say their good-byes, but they will not hand you an owner's manual. As you leave with your newborn the support group collapses behind you, and in the void, parenthood takes on new meaning. What does this cry mean? How can I help my baby get to sleep? What do I do when my baby is sick? Am I caring for my newborn properly? Will I do it wrong? These questions are daunting, but don't panic. God trusts you enough to send your newborn home with you for a lifetime. So be proud. Cherish these historical moments. Your baby's childhood will fast slip away. Soon babies become toddlers and then they will storm through pre-adolescence and become hormonal teens. Before you know it, they will be grown. So take it slow. Sing a few lullabies. Whisper hushes of peace. Let your baby know everything is all right. This will soothe both parent and child.

I remember leaving the hospital—thinking, "Wait, are they going to let me just walk off with him? I don't know beans about babies! I don't have a license to do this."

— *Anne Tyler*

I will certainly hear their cry.

— *Exodus 22:23*

TWO

THE LANGUAGE OF OUR BABY'S CRY

God hears our cries. He keeps our tears in a bottle (Ps 56:8). He knows the meaning behind our cries without hearing our words. But as new parents, we won't understand every cry of our newborn. It's not humanly possible. Each cry may sound the same even though it's a plea for very different things. Your baby will cry for a diaper change, for your presence, because of hunger, or another diaper change. And trying to figure out which cry is which is the chilling task. So remember that it takes time to understand the language of our baby's cry. But soon you will understand your baby as fully as God understands you because every parent learns the language of their baby's cries. God has built this skill into every parent. Sure, there will be times when nothing seems to stop the crying, and if you are unsure of what the baby is crying about, ask another parent or health-care provider to help you understand.

> There never was a child so lovely,
> but his mother was glad to get him asleep.
> — *Ralph Waldo Emerson*

*T*rain a child in the way he should go, and when he is old he will not turn from it.

— *Proverbs 22:6*

THREE
Parenthood: A Quick-Start Guide

*P*romises begin relationships and sustain them when times get tough. It's no different when a child comes into our lives. A new relationship begins. Now we only need to make some promises and parenthood will begin. So promise to protect your children, to nurture their well-being. Promise to get up late at night when it's your turn to change a diaper or to sing a lullaby. Vow that you will never allow anything or anyone to pull you away from perfecting parenthood—not the bills, not lust, not greed, not weariness, nor discouragement of heart.

Promises keep us together when the world tries to rip us apart. For better or for worse. For richer or for poorer. It's no different with a newborn. So make some promises to yourself and to the ones you love. There's no better time to recommit your devotion to God because when we promise to raise our children in the ways of the Lord, they will never depart from it—no matter how far they run. That is God's promise to every new parent.

> Promise a lot and give even more.
> — *Anthony J. D'Angelo*

I am paralyzed with fear.

— *Psalm 143:4, NLT*

FOUR
"Perfection" Is Not a Term in Parenthood

As new parents, we're fearful. It's a big responsibility. We aren't too sure of ourselves. In the beginning, we tremble at our baby's slightest cry. We fret over whether we should be breastfeeding or giving formula. We read every book and search the Internet for the right answers, yet our fear remains.

Sometimes our fear is about us wanting perfection. But perfection is a concept. No one is perfect. The apostle Paul knew this when he wrote, "Aim for perfection" (2 Cor 13:11). He knew perfection is not something humanly possible. But we can aim for it. We can shoot for the stars, but becoming perfect will always be a faraway dream. It's not going to happen in this lifetime.

Sometimes we get tied up in wanting to be perfect and never get around to actually being a parent. Perfection tells us, "I don't think you're ready yet." It tries to paralyze us with fear—fear we will do something wrong. And if we wait until we can do it perfectly, then we'll be waiting a long time. Aim for perfection, but remain grounded.

> You do not need to wait until conditions are perfect.
> — *David J. Schwartz*

She is like a merchant's ship; she brings her food from afar. She gets up before dawn to prepare breakfast for her household and plan the day's work for her servant girls.

— *Proverbs 31:14–15, NLT*

FIVE
COOKING LIKE MARTHA STEWART
WHILE SMILING LIKE KATIE COURIC

*H*ow did she do it? How did the Proverbs 31 woman accomplish such great feats? She's Martha Stewart and Katie Couric all rolled up into one, and most mothers don't measure up to this standard. But you don't have to cook like Martha Stewart while smiling like Katie Couric to be a good parent. No woman has all the virtues.

In this section of Proverbs 31, the first letter of each verse follows the order of the Hebrew alphabet. This device makes it a checklist for virtuous women. But God doesn't expect you to fulfill each one. God only asks that you aspire to Proverbs 31 the way the apostle Paul aimed for perfection. "Not that I have already obtained all this, or have already been made perfect, but I press on to take hold of that for which Christ Jesus took hold of me" (Phil 3:12). So this is the rule for perfection: Let yourself off the Proverbs 31 hook. A virtuous woman is not a perfect one. She's one who loves her family to the best of her ability.

> Who ran to help me when I fell, / And would some pretty story tell, / Or kiss the place to make it well? / My mother.
> — *Ann Taylor*

One day Ruth said to Naomi, "Let me go out into the fields to gather leftover grain behind anyone who will let me do it."

— *Ruth 2:2, NLT*

SIX
PICKING UP AROUND THE HOUSE SHOULDN'T BE A LONELY JOB

*R*uth knew what it meant to pick up after someone. So will you. You'll follow your children's tracks into every room. And strewn around the house will be their toys, clothes, and dirty dishes. And it can feel like you are the only one picking up. When you pick up after your children or your spouse, you are sending a message that it's your job. And they will let you do it.

When you arrive home from the hospital, make a schedule. Split the duties evenly with your spouse. Find a structure where the two of you can compliment one another. Don't do things yourself because you think it's better to just get the task done without arguing or feeling frustrated. We train other people how to treat us.

Remember that you are not alone in parenthood. Others will help if you ask.

> When my kids become wild and unruly, I use a nice,
> safe playpen. When they're finished, I climb out.
> — *Erma Bombeck*

So do not throw away your confidence; it will be richly rewarded.

— *Hebrews 10:35*

SEVEN
Why You Will Never Be a Terrible Parent

Confidence is an important trait as a parent. The Proverbs 31 woman knows what she makes is good. She has confidence. She does not doubt her ability. She doesn't listen to her inner critic—and we all have one. We have the little voice that says, "You are a terrible parent." How we respond to this voice makes all the difference. If we believe this voice, then everything we do is never good enough.

Having confidence isn't a matter of perfection. Confidence means no one else can help fulfill the purpose of your child's life the way you can. Your baby is the sum of all your qualities. This is how you know your child better than anyone else. And it is love that gives us confidence. "Perfect love drives out fear" (1 John 4:18). When we love, we do our best work. And love will always be good enough. It guides us through the storms of life as a rudder turns and guides a ship. "Love never fails" (1 Cor 13:8).

I actually remember feeling delight, at two o'clock in the morning, when the baby woke for his feed because I so longed to have another look at him.

— *Margaret Drabble*

*L*ater she gave birth to a second son and named him Abel. When they grew up, Abel became a shepherd, while Cain was a farmer.

— *Genesis 4:2, NLT*

EIGHT

Throw a Party for Older Siblings

*A*bel carried a slingshot. And Cain dressed in overalls. Abel could count sheep and never get sleepy. But Cain couldn't stand the smell of them. God wires each child differently. And this is the beauty of having children. You get to watch how each one approaches the world. Then you nurture each child accordingly. The mistake would be to show favoritism. So be aware of the signals you send to older children after the birth of a newborn. A new sibling can rock their world. They will feel threatened, as if you have chosen their sibling over them. So take special care in the beginning to reassure your love. Spend moments alone with them, affirming them, so they will feel secure in your love.

The essence of our effort to see that every child has a chance must be to assure each an equal opportunity, not to become equal, but to become different—to realize whatever unique potential of body, mind, and spirit he or she possesses.

— *John Fischer*

I will lie down and sleep in peace, for you alone, O LORD, make me dwell in safety.

— *Psalm 4:8*

NINE
BUILDING TRUST WITH YOUR BABY

Giving birth is a wonderful resolution of nine months of pregnancy. Once you were blind to the growth of your baby inside the womb. But now you see your child. Now you see your baby's facial expressions. Now you watch as your baby stares into your eyes. Your world is different now, and so is your baby's. Everything that went before this moment has changed. Your baby is now an individual in society. No longer inside the chemical exchanges in the womb, your child now receives the exchanges of intimacy in your arms.

Your baby is learning basic trust. She struggles with the question: Will you make me feel secure? She needs to hear your voice and sense your touch. So speak often. Sing lullabies. Caress her face. All of this helps establish new ways to connect with the mother outside the womb. It builds trust. It orientates your baby and gives the sense that everything is safe in this new world.

> Bringing a child into the world is
> the greatest act of hope there is.
> — *Louise Hart*

*L*ove is patient, love is kind. It does not envy, it does not boast, it is not proud. It is not rude, it is not self-seeking, it is not easily angered, it keeps no record of wrongs.

— *1 Corinthians 13:4–5*

TEN
What You'll Talk about When You Talk about Love

A new baby dictates a new schedule. Things will be different. The baby's schedule will consume most of your time and thoughts. You will focus on the baby's schedule more than you will talk to your spouse. So make sure that you don't lose intimacy with him. Make time to be together. Sure, the baby's schedule dictates, but it should never dominate. Learn to be flexible with time together. Communicate. Never assume that your spouse understands why the care of the baby is so time consuming. Set times when the two of you can talk. Make a list of things you would like to talk about with him. By making a list, you bring the issues to light. A common mistake we make is to believe that our spouse can read our minds. No one can. So speak your mind. Communication might not solve everything, but it will give you a clear indication of what is taking place in the heart and mind of your spouse. Never assume you know.

> Effective communication is 20% what you know and 80% how you feel about what you know.
> — *Jim Rohn*

*H*er lamp burns late into the night.

— *Proverbs 31:18, NLT*

ELEVEN

Burning the Candle at Both Ends

Most candles can't burn at both ends. Neither can a parent. Some commentators believe that this verse refers to the Proverbs 31 woman's affluence. She will profit all the days of her life. Others believe it means she has to work deep into the night to accomplish her duties for the day. She should rise early and work late.

This is the rub for the modern parent. How much is enough? How good is good enough? When it comes to our children, we never think we are doing our best or working hard enough for their well-being. But remember that your spiritual well-being requires solitude and rest. And the one thing we can't offer our children when our "lamp burns late into the night," is a calm beginning in the morning, and mornings are important to children. Mornings set the day's pace and mood. Most children who start their day off on the wrong foot will remain anxious throughout the day. So get plenty of rest. You'll need it for the morning dash of getting your children off on the right foot.

> If the knitter is weary the baby will have no new bonnet.
> — *Irish Proverb*

*C*asting the lot settles disputes and keeps strong opponents apart.

— *Proverbs 18:18*

TWELVE
IT'S YOUR TURN TO CHANGE THE DIAPER!

*I*t's a baby's nature to soil diapers, and a parent's duty to change them. But some of the worst disagreements of parenthood take place over the distribution of chores. "Whose turn is it?" When we say, "I've changed more diapers than you," we draw battle lines. Someone wins and someone loses, and the loser usually says, "I may not have changed more diapers, but I've done this, and I've done that." This kind of tit-for-tat is the basis for most arguments. So try not to go there.

Instead of keeping score, designate certain periods throughout the day when you or your spouse will be in charge of certain duties. Keep the periods as short as possible. This way you will feel as if you're working together. The moment you no longer feel as a team, call a meeting and get back on track. Always voice your complaints in a productive way. Keep the communication lines flowing in parenthood. This way no root of bitterness will grow between you.

> The happiest days of my life have been the few which
> I have passed at home in the bosom of my family.
> — *Thomas Jefferson*

I lie down and sleep.

— Psalm 3:5

THIRTEEN
Why Every Parent Should Take a Power Nap

Sleep is a parent's handmaiden. It offers the weary child and the haggard parent the much-needed time apart. But like children, most parents fight sleep. We think about everything we can accomplish. So we turn our child's nap time into activity. We clean the house, watch television, make a few phone calls, or install a new shower curtain. But constant activity may not make you a better parent. In fact, it could hinder your productivity.

One *Psychology Today* article discusses studies done on workers who take power naps. It concluded that well-rested workers had "greater alertness, faster reaction times, better problem-solving, and increased creativity." And what our child needs most is a well-rested parent. So be smart. Don't waste the one good helper you can depend on. Get the most from your handmaiden. Take a power nap. Let sleep revitalize child and parent.

> Rock'd in the cradle of the deep,
> I lay me down in peace to sleep.
> — *Emma Willard*

We do not enjoy being disciplined. It is painful at the time, but later, after we have learned from it, we have peace, because we start living in the right way.

— *Hebrews 12:11*

FOURTEEN
Obsessing over Discipline

Only you can decide how to discipline your child. Others will have opinions, and they will share them. They will tell you how they raised their child. Some will be pro-punishment. Others will think punishment is the crime. And there will be principles you'll like, and other ones you will hate with a passion. The key is to do research and discover which ones work best for you. For some, "time out" is the discipline of choice. Others may take away privileges or toys.

Many paths lead to discipline. Eventually you will have to choose one. Discipline changes the relationship between you and your child. But being prepared will lessen the pain when it happens—hopefully. Because before you know it your baby will become a toddler, and toddlers get into mischief.

Having a plan will lessen the initial wound you will feel as a disciplinarian. And in the end both parent and child will discover peace. It keeps our children living in the right way. It may be difficult, but it is not bad.

> Without discipline, there's no life at all.
> — *Katharine Hepburn*

Why are you downcast, O my soul? Why so disturbed within me? Put your hope in God, for I will yet praise him, my Savior and my God.

— *Psalm 42:5–6*

FIFTEEN
How to Get the Funk Out

*K*ing David had a way of talking himself out of a funk. He said, "Why are you downcast, O my soul?" He used self-talk. He lifted his burdens by speaking to his soul. And there will be times when our children must talk themselves out of a trial or a difficulty. They will have downcast moments that dictate how they think and feel. Self-talk is like lifting one's soul by the bootstraps of will. This is not a bad thing. If it works, we should be wise enough to follow David's example.

So instill in your child the art of self-talk. One of the ways we do this is by using encouraging statements. Tell your child, "You can do this." "You're smart." "Don't give up." "Keep trying." Internalizing these statements will help lift them out of their own funk someday. These statements will offer strength. So use them repeatedly. There's no better time to start than now. Even infants need comforting words.

> Relentless, repetitive self-talk is what changes our self-image.
> — *Denis Waitley*

And when your children ask you, "What does this ceremony mean to you?" then tell them, "It is the Passover sacrifice to the LORD."

— *Exodus 12:26–27*

SIXTEEN

OH! THE QUESTIONS THEY WILL ASK

Children are full of questions. It's as if their little glands produce them. Then they feel if they don't ask them, their heads might spin. So they ask. They wonder why the sky is blue, why the earth is round, and why birds fly. And these are the easy questions before the big one: "Where do babies come from?" That's always the tricky one.

But when our children ask about the church and about its ceremonies, make sure they get the answers. Tell them from your heart what these ceremonies mean to you. Then let the church teach them. It is a parent's responsibility. If you're careless about the church and its ceremonies, then they won't bother to ask. But when it becomes intriguing to them because it is intriguing to you, you have a captivated audience. Jesus said, "Let the little children come to me" (Matt 19:14). And you know they hit him with questions. They probably brought a smile to his face. Can't you hear him chuckle?

> You know children are growing up when
> they start asking questions that have answers.
> — *John J. Plomp*

That was why his parents said, "He is of age; ask him."

— *John 9:23*

SEVENTEEN

Children Are a Gift from God

*T*he beautiful thing about the parents in this reading is how they take ownership of the boy they could have easily denied. He was of legal age to fend for himself. "He is of age; ask him." It wasn't that they were denying him as a son. They respected the boundaries of their relationship with him. They refused to speak for him. They let his involvement with Christ remain between Christ and him.

Most parents these days would have spoken for him to save his hide at the demise of their own. But they had their own life, and so will you one day. Then there will be boundaries you must honor. Parents forget this along the way. They forget that even though we have sons and daughters given to us as a gift from God, they are ultimately his gift we give back. Children grow up, and we must let them. So make that commitment now. Always keep in the back of your mind this one rule: "My child will be of legal age one day, and I will have to step away from his affairs."

> Human beings are the only creatures
> that allow their children to come back home.
> — *Bill Cosby*

*T*une your ears to wisdom, and concentrate on understanding.

— *Exodus 12:26–27*

EIGHTEEN
Don't Be Afraid to Analyze Your Child

Charles Steinmetz was an electrical engineering genius who worked for General Electric. After his retirement, GE was baffled about the breakdown of a complex of machinery, so they asked Charles to pinpoint the problem. He walked around the machines, then took a piece of chalk and made a big cross mark on one particular machine. To their amazement, it turned out to be the precise location of the breakdown. Steinmetz sent a bill to GE for $10,000—a staggering sum in the early part of the twentieth century. So, they asked him to itemize it. He wrote back:

Making one cross mark: $1.00

Knowing where to put it: $9,999.00

Children need the diagnostic love of parents—not that we can totally fix them. But we can direct them to the One who can. This is the ultimate hope of a parent.

Curiosity has its own reasons for existing. One cannot help but be in awe when he contemplates the mysteries of eternity, of life, of the marvelous structure of reality. Never lose a holy curiosity.

— *Albert Einstein*

"*N*either this man nor his parents sinned," said Jesus, "but this happened so that the work of God might be displayed in his life."

"We know he is our son," the parents answered, "and we know he was born blind."

— John 9:3, 20

NINETEEN

THE MYSTERY OF HANDICAPPED CHILDREN

The parents of this son knew the pain and surprise of a son being born blind. Birth defects and disabilities are a mystery. We don't know why some things happen. We don't know why God allows pain in this world. It's beyond our comprehension. But it hurts to see our children suffering. We feel helpless. Sometimes we play the "If I had only…" game. We question every aspect of the pregnancy. But Jesus told the Pharisees that neither his father nor his mother were responsible for his blindness (John 9:3). And this stands as the answer to every parent who somehow feels responsible for a birth defect. It doesn't lessen the pain. But God increases his glory in them. How? Maybe it causes us to love deeper. Who knows? But God doesn't need any kind of defect to accomplish his good and receive glory. He's not into pain for what he can get out of it. But, rather, he brings good from it. God makes no mistakes, even when it makes no sense. The mystery of the world will always be with us.

> I thank God for my handicaps, for, through them,
> I have found myself, my work, and my God.
> — *Helen Keller*

How long, O LORD?
—❖—

— Psalm 13:1

TWENTY
How Long, O Lord?

*P*arenthood has its stages. Children develop and with each stage we cry, "How much longer, O Lord?" Here are the three prominent stages that seem as though they will never end:

1. Sleepless nights
2. Mystery crying
3. Diaper changing

If we are not careful we can let these stages smother the joy of parenthood. Don't see these as stages of endurance, rather think of them as passing moments of joy. These stages are temporary. They will pass. So never just endure what should bring happiness, no matter how tough the circumstance. And if your joy has depleted, say to yourself, "This too shall pass." And it will. Trust me.

> The best thing about the future is that
> it comes only one day at a time.
> — *Abraham Lincoln*

From the lips of children and infants you have ordained praise.

— *Psalm 8:2*

TWENTY-ONE
Out of the Mouths of Babes

*E*xactly what comes out of the mouths of children and babies that praises God? No one is quite sure. No one knows what coos, gurgles, and babbling means in the ears of the Heavenly Father. But He has ordained it. Maybe their innocent and smiling faces warm the heart of God. We will never be certain. But our children produce ordained praise. This is how important your child is to God. He loves to listen to our children. He calls it the worship from earth that reaches heaven.

Maybe today you are tired. Maybe you haven't had much sleep. Take a moment sometime today, and listen to your child's ordained praise. Let the gurgles, babble, or coos wash over you. Listen and rejoice. Let this bring a smile to your weary face. God, the maker of the universe, takes delight in the noises of our children. How astonishing that God should think of them in this way!

> For every child that is born, it brings with it the hope that God is not yet disappointed with man.
> — *Rabindranath Tagore*

*Y*ou shall assign to them as their responsibility all they are to carry.

— *Numbers 4:27*

TWENTY-TWO
Don't Forget about Yourself

*P*arents carry a heavy load of responsibility. For most of us, we have only been responsible for a spouse and for ourselves. But now we are responsible for a life other than our own. We no longer have time for pleasurable activities. Hobbies get eliminated. Weekly lunch dates with friends are postponed. To be honest, most everything is postponed that doesn't focus on the new baby. In the beginning this seems honorable and necessary. It's our responsibility to do everything for the well-being of our children. But if we are not careful, we can burn out. Make sure to include some downtime in your schedule. Incorporate a hobby into your routine. Start scrapbooking. Join a book club. Reward yourself with a bowl of ice cream. Do something that brings you pleasure. You deserve it.

You learn to give up or postpone many of the pleasures you enjoyed, such as eating when you are hungry, watching a movie all the way through, going to sleep when you are tired.
— *Lydia Davis*

Later she gave birth to a second son and named him Abel.

— *Genesis 4:2, NLT*

TWENTY-THREE
How to Lose the Post-Pregnancy Weight

Getting Cain out of diapers and into fig leaves was a major event. Eve was exhausted. Then Abel was born. And Eve was no longer the rebellious girl with the perfect figure, picking fruit from the forbidden tree. Giving birth had taken its toll. She was up two fig-leaf sizes since getting pregnant with Abel. And she didn't have time for jogging through the garden in the cool of the evening. But she didn't like her reflection in the pool, either.

Some moms struggle with their post-pregnancy weight. One easy way to exercise is to go for a stroll. Find a friend who wants to lose weight, too. This will keep you motivated while allowing you to socialize. As the weight comes off, you'll feel better about yourself. The health of your baby relies on you taking care of yourself—mentally and physically. So take it slow. Take it one step at a time. The weight will come off as you work at it each day.

The baby was a lovely little boy, but sad to say, he did not weigh sixty pounds. That is what I had gained and that was what I had to lose.

— *Barbara Bush*

A man's steps are directed by the LORD. How then can anyone understand his own way?

— *Proverbs 20:24*

TWENTY-FOUR
A Parent's Prayer

*P*arenthood is one hurried moment to the next task. Sometimes our plans get botched and things don't go as planned. At the start of the day, take five minutes, and open your Bible to the Lord's Prayer (Matt 6:9–13). Pray:

Our Father in heaven, hallowed be your name,
your kingdom come, your will be done on earth as it is in heaven.
Give us today our daily bread.
Forgive us our debts, as we also have forgiven our debtors.
And lead us not into temptation, but deliver us from the evil one. Amen.

Fill your day with the first part of the prayer. Throughout the day, repeat: "Your will be done." This principle frees us from placing expectations on our day. Sure, we plan the day. But things may not go as planned. This is when we understand that we make the plans, but God directs our steps. So be flexible. Say, "Your will be done."

Very often when I haven't faith in my faith, I have to have faith in His faith. He makes me believe in myself and my possibilities, when I simply can't.

— E. Stanley Jones

Let your word agree with theirs, and speak favorably.

— *1 Kings 22:13*

TWENTY-FIVE
Teaching Our Children about God

*A*greeing on the spirituality of our children can cause friction in our marriage and ultimately in our children. Some spouses could care less what our children believe, and this is where the trouble lies. You will need complete support from your spouse to teach your children in the ways of the Lord. Being at odds about this neutralizes what the church teaches. It undermines the Lord's authority.

There is probably no other stressor like this one. So, sit down with your spouse and find some middle ground. Ask questions. "Are you against our children attending church?" "Will you help me raise them in the ways of the Lord?" If your spouse can't support your beliefs, then ask him to support you and your desire to raise your children in the church. This may be the only thing you'll agree upon. But it's a start.

> A hypocrite is the kind of politician who would cut down a redwood tree, then mount the stump and make a speech for conservation.
> — *Adlai Stevenson*

*T*hen he entered the temple area and began driving out those who were selling.

— *Luke 19:45*

TWENTY-SIX

A Parent's Frustration Level

*E*veryone loses his or her cool sometimes. Jesus did. But chasing moneychangers from the temple is righteous indignation, not explosive anger. So we can't use this incident as license to explode. Parents usually lose their tempers because of frustration. We get frustrated when our children continually disobey, so we dole out extreme punishment and ground them for life. Stress that builds up becomes extreme frustration, which can lead to explosive anger, so know your frustration limits.

Usually we can feel our frustration level rising. Our patience becomes short. We yell more often. We snap, too. We go from giving warnings to screaming threats. This is how we know we've crossed over from frustration to anger, so heed the warning signs. Maintain self-control. Don't let your actions become regretful mistakes. Learn to defuse your frustration. Take walks. Pray. Write in a journal. Call a friend. Learn to ventilate your frustration before it builds to anger.

> Anger, if not restrained, is frequently more hurtful to us than the injury that provokes it.
> — *Seneca*

*T*he righteous care about justice for the poor, but the wicked have no such concern.

— *Proverbs 29:7*

TWENTY-SEVEN

How to Drive Selfishness from Your Child

*J*esus said the poor will always be with us (Mark 14:7). They are a constant reminder that justice in the world is off kilter. This is why good people should care. The poor need us. They need our time and attention. So teach your child at an early age to care for the poor. It lets her know that life can always be worse. Hopefully, it will cause her to appreciate what she has even more. You can do this by regularly donating old clothes and toys. Over time, children become emotionally attached to their clothes and toys. And giving them away will open their eyes to someone else's perspective. It teaches them empathy and encourages growth in virtues.

Take things you no longer need to a shelter. Tell your child the reasoning behind it. Let her put her things in a bag separate from your own. Then allow her to hand it over to the shelter. It will make a lasting impression. You never want your child to grow up without awareness and empathy for the poor.

> Modesty and unselfishness—these are virtues
> which men praise—and pass by.
> — *André Maurois*

*H*is eyes will be darker than wine, his teeth whiter than milk.

— *Genesis 49:12*

TWENTY-EIGHT
Cutting Teeth and Gnawing on Toys

Cutting teeth is not a fun part of parenthood. Most babies begin cutting teeth between four and seven months old. And they will cry and chew on things. They will be irritable. So use distraction tools. Take a walk. Go to the park. Provide as much stimuli as possible to grab their attention. Teething rings work well. A wet washcloth is worth a try, as well. You can also try massaging their gums. Talk with your doctor about using teething gel or some other kind of pain reliever.

But know that this stage passes. You can only endure it. So tackle this stage with the greatest of endurance. "Therefore, as God's chosen people, holy and dearly loved, clothe yourselves with compassion, kindness, humility, gentleness and patience" (Col 3:12).

> To endure is the first thing that a child ought to learn,
> and that which he will have the most need to know.
> — *Jean Jacques Rousseau*

$\mathcal{D}$o not let the sun go down while you are still angry.

— *Ephesians 4:26*

TWENTY-NINE
What to Do before You Sleep

New parents will discover fresh ways to quarrel. We argue because we are tired and need rest; because we are frustrated with other aspects of our lives; or simply because we are trying to adjust to the new dimension of our marriage. But before you sleep, work things out between the two of you. People who sleep on anger wake up in a pouty mood and carry yesterday's anger into today. They ruminate anger like cows chewing a cud. And when cows finally swallow the cud, it's not the end of it. Sometimes the cud is regurgitated to repeat the process. And we know that has to taste nasty.

Start each day with a clean slate. Don't allow your anger to seethe. If you do, eventually it will become bitterness. This is why the apostle Paul wrote, "Get rid of all bitterness, rage and anger, brawling and slander, along with every form of malice. Be kind and compassionate to one another, forgiving each other, just as in Christ God forgave you" (Eph 4:31–32).

> The only fool bigger than the person who knows it all
> is the person who argues with him.
> — *Stanislaw Lec*

𝒟o not fear the reproach of men or be terrified by their insults.

— *Isaiah 51:7*

THIRTY
HAS YOUR CHILD MET THE MIGHTY MILESTONES?

Milestones can become an insult to some. Upon hearing how well other children are doing, they feel slighted by God. But some babies advance more quickly than others. Slow development doesn't always mean something is wrong. Some babies crawl at a certain age while others are walking. Some babble while another child of the same age is speaking in short sentences. But the hardest thing to hear and to see is how other children are meeting these milestones when your child is not. If you fear something is wrong, then make an appointment with your pediatrician. And, remember, every baby has his or her threshold of development.

If a child lives with tolerance, he learns to be patient. If a child lives with encouragement he learns confidence. If a child lives with praise, he learns to appreciate. He a child lives with fairness, he learns justice. If a child lives with security, he learns to have faith. If a child lives with approval, he learns to like himself. If a child lives with acceptance and friendship, he learns to find love in the world. With what is your child living?

— *Dorothy Law Nolte*

My son, preserve sound judgment and discernment, do not let them out of your sight.

— *Proverbs 3:21*

THIRTY-ONE
SAFETY FIRST, SAFETY LAST, SAFETY ALWAYS

For Thomas

When it comes to safety, it seems we've lost our minds. Nothing is safe anymore. Everything has a warning label these days. A Superman costume has this label: Wearing of this garment does not enable you to fly. A hair dryer has this warning label: Do not use while sleeping. A warning label on a car sun shield: Do not drive with shield in place.

Have companies gone crazy? Are lawsuits that prevalent? While we appreciate warning labels, some seem superfluous. Our child will probably never don a Superman costume and jump off the house, thinking he can fly. But we are safety conscious in America, which is good. Safety first, safety last, safety always.

Have sound judgment. Have common sense. But realize that many harmful things escape common sense. They become too familiar. So here's a warning for reading this devotional: Removing words will make this unreadable. Really, be careful. Things lurk out there.

> Early and provident fear is the mother of safety.
> — *Edmund Burke*

Your eyes saw my unformed body. All the days ordained for me were written in your book before one of them came to be.

— *Psalm 139:16*

THIRTY-TWO
The Days of Their Lives

*I*t's wild to think God has the days of our children's lives planned. He knows their first words. He knows when they will crawl, and then walk. Maybe the Great Artist has created an illustrated picture book. Maybe he illustrates their first day of school. Maybe he has a picture of them falling, and then getting up, or maybe their first words are printed at the bottom of a page.

We will see this great book one day. But for now, we allow the pages of their lives to unfold. We do it with confidence. We do it with total trust. God is the great conductor of their lives. We are only his handmaidens and servants. We have been chosen to raise our children according to what he has written in the book. When they grow older, we give them back. It has all been written down. Now the wonderful task has begun. Sit for a few minutes and think about your child's life. Where will he or she be in five years? In ten years? In twenty years? How will you help God get them there?

> You know your children are growing up when they stop asking where they came from and refuse to tell you where they're going.
> — *P. J. O'Rourke*

*I*f you had responded to my rebuke, I would have poured out my heart to you and made my thoughts known to you.

— *Proverbs 1:23*

THIRTY-THREE
How to Use Your Child's Middle Name

Children don't always respond to verbal threats or what the proverb calls rebukes. Their nonchalance is because we've threatened more than we've disciplined. So stand behind your threats. Never ground your child for a week, only to reverse it two days later. Once you do this, you have undermined you parental authority. You've conditioned your child to think, "Mom will change her mind. She always does this when she grounds me."

Don't use empty threats. They know you'll never stick to them. Once they realize our words are empty, they stop listening. And it doesn't help to threaten with bolts of lightning from heaven. They know the lightning won't strike. So just use their middle name. It has worked since the dawn of time. It will clue them in to the fact that we are serious.

> Any child can tell you that the sole purpose of a middle name
> is so he can tell when he's really in trouble.
> — *Dennis Fakes*

𝒯he godly give good advice to their friends; the wicked lead them astray.

— *Proverbs 12:26, NLT*

THIRTY-FOUR
Where to Go for Advice

New parents are targets for advice. Almost everyone you meet is an expert on raising children, and they don't mind passing the information along. They will also let you know just how remarkable their children are. It gets old really fast.

Good advice usually comes from godly friends. They listen. They ask the right questions. Then they offer what you need to hear. Godly friends don't make you feel like a rookie. They let you know they are on the journey with you. We need people we can turn to in our moments of need. We need friends who will be honest with us. Godly friends teach us how to be a good person and a good person always makes a great parent. So get involved at church. Join a group. Help in the nursery. Network with other parents and get on the journey with them.

When we honestly ask ourselves which persons in our lives mean the most to us, we often find that it is those who, instead of giving advice, solutions, or cures, have chosen rather to share our pain and touch our wounds with a warm and tender hand.

— *Henri Nouwen*

My friends have forgotten me.

— *Job 19:14*

THIRTY-FIVE
MODIFYING THE TERMS OF FRIENDSHIP

Nothing changes our social life like having a baby. And many times being a parent interferes with our friendships.

Some single friends may feel forgotten by you, so include them when you can. Maybe get a babysitter. Go see a movie with them. Or if you can't leave your baby, go to lunch and take the baby along. They would love to see the new you. But don't spend all of your time talking non-stop about your child. They probably don't care how many diapers you've changed or what your pediatrician said.

Sometimes single friends think we are overdoing it as a parent when we don't stay out late with our kids. They don't understand the need to keep children on a schedule. So, don't expect them to understand your parenting style. But be their friend as you always have, even if you have to modify the terms of your friendship.

At the end of your life, you will never regret not having passed one more test, not winning one more verdict, or not closing one more deal. You will regret time not spent with a husband, a friend, a child, or a parent.

— *Barbara Bush*

How I hated discipline.

— *Proverbs 5:12*

THIRTY-SIX
Setting Speed Limits for Your Child

No one delights in speed limit laws. No one wakes in the morning and shouts, "I can't wait to obey the speed limit on the way to work!" It just doesn't happen because anytime we face a law, we lose a sense of freedom. And whenever we discipline our children, we restrict their freedom.

Some parents get caught in the trap of trying to make their children happy at all costs. This practice is a disservice. Eventually, our children will face responsibility outside our domain. Teachers want them to remain quiet while they teach. Policemen won't overlook a speeding violation. If a parent won't hold his child accountable, society will. This is the reason we have such heartache in the world.

When we raise our children without discipline and a sense of responsibility, then we make them believe they are above the laws of the land. Our children may not know better, but as parents, we should. Love your children enough to discipline them.

Discipline is the soul of an army. It makes small numbers formidable; procures success to the weak; and esteem to all.
— *George Washington*

Command those who are rich in this present world not to be arrogant nor to put their hope in wealth, which is so uncertain, but to put their hope in God, who richly provides us with everything for our enjoyment.

— 1 Timothy 6:17

THIRTY-SEVEN
Being Rich Is Not a Sin

*B*eing rich is not a sin. But any blessing can become a curse. It happens when our riches possess us, instead of us possessing riches. It happens when our riches make us arrogant. This is what Paul is warning Timothy against. And if we're not careful we can teach our children that security comes from wealth. But as Paul warns, we should teach our children that God provides us with everything we need for enjoyment because the world's system will teach them enjoyment comes from being rich and acting snobby. Jesus said, "What good will it be for a man if he gains the whole world, yet forfeits his soul?" (Matt 16:26).

So teach your children the importance of making a living, but never make riches the goal of life. Safeguard against the possibility that they might forfeit their soul for wealth.

> There's no reason to be the richest man in the cemetery.
> You can't do any business from there.
> — *Colonel Harland Sanders*

𝒟o not hold against us the sins of the fathers; may your mercy come quickly to meet us, for we are in desperate need.

— *Psalm 79:8*

THIRTY-EIGHT
Who Said You'd Become like Your Mother?

Our parents have left indelible marks upon our character. We take these traits into our own parenthood. We find ourselves disciplining our children the way our parents disciplined us. We say the same things. We dole out the same punishment. We encourage our children the way they encouraged us. Sometimes it's automatic. We haven't planned to use our parents' lines. Other times we know exactly what we're doing. We're doing it our parents' way because it worked with us.

But you may use their bad parenting, too. For some, this is a great fear. Maybe your parents weren't the best role models. Maybe they embarrassed you. Now, as a parent, you want to do a better job and never humiliate your child. How will your actions affect her character? Will she have the self-esteem you never had? Probably. Why? Because you made use of the bad parenting to become a better parent. You've turned it into something positive. It's how you choose to use what you've been taught by your parents.

> Sooner or later we all quote our mothers.
> — *Bern Williams*

Restore to me the joy of your salvation and grant me a willing spirit, to sustain me.

— *Exodus 12:26*

THIRTY-NINE

The Willingness to Succeed as a Parent

Willingness is half the battle. We must be willing to stay strong. We have many more developmental stages to go in our child's life. Diapers will not last. Toddlers will grow up. Teeth become molars. Crying becomes the longing for some boy or girl. Then, they turn sixteen and take to the highway. Then college. What do we need to say about that? We need God to grant us the spirit of willingness to sustain us. Life moves fast.

Parenthood, like any enterprise, has to be helped along. It doesn't happen by merely thinking about it. Willingness comes to those who say, "I can do this." Pope John XXIII said, "It is easier for a father to have children than for children to have a real father." Willingness is the desire to be the real father, a better parent. Be an example. This is at the heart of what a good parent does.

> Children have never been very good at listening to their elders, but they have never failed to imitate them.
> — *James Baldwin*

Declare to my people their rebellion.

— *Isaiah 58:1*

FORTY
Parents Rule!

All children hate rules. They think they should be allowed to stay up as late as they want and get up when they want. They want to play at school and sleep in church. Our kids have it easy these days. King Edward VIII once said, "The thing that impresses me the most about America is the way parents obey their children." He has a point. We tend to pacify our children instead of teaching them boundaries and rules. But responsibility is something they can learn now or later when they get put in detention for disobeying at school. No parent wants that.

Sit down and make some rules you want your children to abide by. Teach them to be respectful. Expect them to obey early in childhood, and it will stick. You have the power to pacify or to be in control, and remember that if you don't control your child, they will control you.

America's future will be determined by the home and the school. The child becomes largely what it is taught, hence we must watch what we teach it, and how we live before it.
— Jane Addams

Many are the plans in a man's heart, but it is the LORD's purpose that prevails.

— *Proverbs 19:21*

FORTY-ONE
The Plans We Make May Not Be the Way They Choose

*P*arents are notorious for making plans. We want our children to attend the finest schools. Maybe even follow our example and choose the same career. We want our children to become doctors, Pulitzer prize-winning scholars, or researchers who discover the cure for cancer. But our dreams should never be greater than the Lord's plans for their lives. The Lord may want them to be a firefighter instead of a doctor. He may want them to be a professor of physics instead of a lawyer.

Allow your children to follow the path of their choosing, which means we must trust God will lead them. There will always be the temptation to prod them. But there is a way to get involved. Try to understand the gifts God has given your child. Take notice of certain traits. Then when they get the harebrained idea to become a professional reality show contestant, you can give them a reality check. Point out the way God has gifted them. Until then, do your research.

> You were born to win, but to be a winner, you must plan to win, prepare to win, and expect to win.
> — *Zig Ziglar*

He will yet fill your mouth with laughter and your lips with shouts of joy.

— *Job 8:21*

FORTY-TWO
Quit Being so Serious

*T*here's a time for everything: a time to be foolish and a time to be serious. And foolishness can be funny and cute. Playing around with our children creates memorable moments. We love the way they laugh when they get tickled. The way they want us to tickle them again and again. Acting crazy is fun. This is good foolishness. So make some time to be foolish. Some parents have a hard time with this. We can be so serious. We worry about our jobs, about sales, about where the money is going to come from. Too much seriousness drives the joy from our children. So lighten up. Get down on the floor. Roll around. Be silly. Have some fun. It endears your child to you. You're down on their level.

> He dares to be a fool, and that is the first step
> in the direction of wisdom.
> — *James Gibbons Huneker*

My son, pay attention to what I say; listen closely to my words.

— *Proverbs 4:20*

FORTY-THREE
How to Mean What You Say and Say What You Mean

*I*t's every parent's hope that our children will take our advice and use it. But wisdom is hard to teach. We gain it over time, so plan for the long haul on this one. Find creative ways to teach your wisdom. Do it each day in different ways as your children progress through different stages of childhood. Games work well with younger children. Any time you can teach them and have fun doing it, they will learn. As they get older write notes. Stick a quote from someone you admire in their lunch boxes. E-mail encouraging words to them. But keep it short. The simpler the better, and always make it heartfelt. "For wisdom will enter your heart, and knowledge will be pleasant to your soul" (Prov 2:10).

> In teaching you cannot see the fruit of a day's work.
> It is invisible and remains so, maybe for twenty years.
> — *Jacques Barzun*

Though they stumble, they will never fall, for the Lord holds them by the hand.

— *Psalm 37:24, NLT*

FORTY-FOUR
The Amazing Promise to Every Parent

*T*his psalm is an amazing promise to every parent. It's a wonderful picture, so visualize your child with the Lord. See his mighty hand. See the way it holds your child's tiny one. It's real even though we can't see it. His hand is there holding theirs; keeping them from falling. And it will be there long after we're gone. It will be there when we fail to see it. So never doubt it.

May we be the same kind of parent. Let's be there for our children in any kind of weather. Be a strong advocate for your child. Assume nothing. Always check out every program they are involved with on every level. The times are tough. Predators prowl. People aren't always what they seem. Check them out. Hold your child's hand. Make it known that you are a concerned parent. Deceivers don't like the strong. They search out the weak. So always be a strong presence. And never forget who's ultimately holding their hand.

> I know God will not give me anything I can't handle.
> I just wish that he didn't trust me so much.
> — *Mother Teresa*

A heart at peace gives life to the body.

— *Proverbs 14:30*

FORTY-FIVE

To Breastfeed or Not to Breastfeed

To breastfeed or not to breastfeed is a huge dilemma these days. Everybody seems to have an opinion. And it can be so confusing. We even tell ourselves, "If breastfeeding doesn't work out, it's not a big deal—I'll switch to formula." But this always lurks as a cop-out in the back of our minds. We feel weak—even though it's not true. We feel we are doing a disservice to our baby. We feel guilty when the women in our lives say, "Breast is best." But there is so much conflicting data on the issue. So we have to find our own peace about it.

Either way you choose will mean a healthy baby. Go with your instincts. You're the parent. Make the decision that you feel is right for your baby—and you. Then stick to it. In five years, no one is going to walk up to your child and say, "You look like a formula baby," or "You look like a breastfed baby." So don't make yourself sick over it. Choose what's best for your situation.

> Never go to your high school reunion pregnant, or they will think that is all you have done since you graduated.
> — *Erma Bombeck*

*E*njoy life with your wife, whom you love.

— *Ecclesiastes 9:9*

FORTY-SIX

Adventures in Babysitting

*M*ost dates with your spouse will now involve a babysitter. The night will begin with your child clinging to your leg and screaming. You will have second thoughts. You will have the urge to comfort your child, but it rarely works. They just get louder. But you have to get over it. The night out with your spouse will do more good than staying home. So don't be afraid to leave your child with a babysitter whom you trust.

Sometimes our marriages suffer when we give in to parenting guilt. Don't let this happen. Give your marriage the break it deserves. You need intimacy. So get a babysitter. Then trust them. Enjoy yourself. The two of you need time alone.

> Having a child is surely the most beautifully irrational act
> that two people in love can commit.
> — *Bill Cosby*

*I*nstead, I devoted myself to the work on this wall.

— *Nehemiah 5:16*

FORTY-SEVEN
SHOULD YOU WORK OR STAY AT HOME?

*Y*ou'll face the decision to work or not to work. Sure, two incomes makes things easier. But then again, you're missing time with your child. It's a tough decision with no easy answer.

Census figures show 54 percent of mothers with a graduate or professional degree no longer work full time. This statistic alarms some who believe the workforce is suffering because of it. But it's not wrong to want to stay at home. Nor is it wrong to desire a career. God is silent on the issue. And maybe what Saint Augustine said applies here, "Love God, and do what you like." Work is your choice. But sometimes it's an economical hardship. We must work to make ends meet. If you are in this category, then work out a plan to stay at home, if that's what you want. Or remain in your line of work, if that's what you want. The choice is yours. And there will always be those who won't like your decision either way. So just do it.

> Motherhood has a very humanizing effect.
> Everything gets reduced to essentials.
> — *Meryl Streep*

And nd my God will meet all your needs according to his glorious riches in Christ Jesus.

— *Philippians 4:19*

FORTY-EIGHT
BILLS! BILLS! BILLS!
DEALING WITH THE MONEY CRUNCH

*I*t costs a lot of money to raise a son or a daughter. Some may think daughters cost more. Maybe the wedding is the deciding bill. Who knows? Maybe you've been surprised with twins or triplets. They abound these days. Maybe you've lost your job. Maybe you face the decision to stay at home or return to work. Whatever you face, never make decisions based solely on money. Sure, some financial decisions leave you no choice. But some decisions rest in the hands of God, the great decision maker. Sometimes we must risk and trust him. He can open doors no one can shut. He can close doors no one can open. So relax. Even though money is an issue, it doesn't always have the last word. God knows your needs. Jesus said, "Look at the birds of the air; they do not sow or reap or store away in barns, and yet your heavenly Father feeds them. Are you not much more valuable than they?" (Matt 6:26–27).

> The world is full of people looking for spectacular happiness while they snub contentment.
> — *Doug Larson*

My lover is mine, and I am his.

— *Song of Songs 2:16*

FORTY-NINE
How to Fall in Love Again

*P*romises built your marriage—promises to love in sickness and in health and for richer or for poorer. These promises were sweeter than honey on your wedding day. Now time has passed. Your child is born. Maybe you've reached financial freedom. Or maybe you are struggling to make ends meet. Sometimes promises hurt. People let us down. But it's hard to argue with the promises we've made. They are unchangeable. They will never deteriorate and become nonexistent.

Promises are more than psychology, more than happiness or sadness, even though promises contain all of these. Promises are what you return to when you've lost your way. They bring marriages back together. They preserve relationships. A promise is the glue of love. It holds love together when love doesn't feel so good. For it is love that made you say those promises on your wedding day. And the spark of your relationship resides in those promises. So remember your vows. This is how you fall in love again.

> You know it's true love when you can't believe
> you ever lived without it.
> — *Katherine Seelig*

*M*eanwhile, the people in Judah said, "The strength of the laborers is giving out, and there is so much rubble that we cannot rebuild the wall."

— *Nehemiah 4:10*

FIFTY
FEEL OVERWHELMED?

For Martha and Suzanne

*P*arenthood started with a loud cry from your baby and everyone cheered. But everyone is gone now and reality is sinking in. You realize being a parent is hard. It costs. It demands. And mostly you are just tired. You're overwhelmed. This happened to Nehemiah when he was rebuilding the walls around Jerusalem. When the people hit the halfway point, they became exhausted and discouraged. But, they trusted in God. They refocused their energies and determined to complete the work.

Don't get frustrated. Get proactive. Ask yourself, "How can I receive help?" Make a list of things people can do—even if it's to fold a basket of laundry. Don't be too prideful to reach out for help. Friends have offered. Family has, too. So help is just a phone call away. Ask. Your baby's growth depends on your health. So pace yourself. Don't get overwhelmed.

> Slow and steady wins the race.
> — *Aesop*

When you pass through the waters, I will be with you; and when you pass through the rivers, they will not sweep over you. When you walk through the fire, you will not be burned; the flames will not set you ablaze.

— *Isaiah 43:2*

FIFTY-ONE
The Wrong Occupation for Every Mother

*M*others are known for worrying. They worry that disaster is lurking around every corner. They worry about their children's eating habits. They worry about their friends. They worry about their souls, about their involvement in church. They want the best of everything—as it should be. But worrying takes on a negative role when worry is combined with fear. Worrying can become a mother's occupation when she fears the world more than she trusts God.

When we trust the Lord for protection, we leave things that are out of our control in his hands. He can move mountains. He raises the dead. He feeds the multitudes. He heals the sick. He is our protection in troubling times. So pray for your children instead of worrying about them. "The eternal God is your refuge, and underneath are the everlasting arms" (Deut 33:27). We may not see his arms, but they are there. Our children will not fall. There's no need to worry.

> Our times are in His hand Who saith, "A whole I planned,
> Youth shows but half; trust God: See all, nor be afraid!"
> — *Robert Browning*

Surely my husband will love me now.

— *Genesis 29:32*

FIFTY-TWO
Shoot the Bull with Your Spouse

Most women don't feel attractive after giving birth. You may feel fat or tired or both. You may not want your husband to look at your body. This is normal. But don't hide your feelings along with your body. Tell your spouse how you are feeling. Men don't get it sometimes. They can't see through to what bothers mothers with newborns—and they can't read minds. Sometimes men lose their sensitivity. So help your husband out. Speak about what's going on inside you. Communication is important after the birth of your baby. Make sure to discuss your problems, your emotions, and your appearance for at least ten minutes every day. This ten-minute bull session could be the key to marriage in the post-pregnancy stage. So only talk about each other. This bull session is about your romance. Rekindle it. Take ten minutes a day.

> If pregnancy were a book,
> they would cut the last two chapters.
> — *Nora Ephron*

*T*en times now you have reproached me.

—*Job 19:3*

FIFTY-THREE
What a Father Should Never Do

*A*dam may have been the first nagging father. There's no way to know, but he could have nagged.

Adam: "Have you gathered wood for your mother yet?"
Son: "No, sir. I'm waiting on the rain to stop."
Adam: "Did I tell you to wait until the rain stopped?"
Son: "No, sir."
Adam: "Well move it."

We know Adam wasn't perfect, nor will we be. We carry a lot of dysfunction into fatherhood. And if we are not careful our sons will pass it on to their sons. So don't nag and exasperate. Teach. Approach your son with love and treat his shortcomings with patience.

When I was a boy of fourteen, my father was so ignorant I could hardly stand to have the old man around. But when I got to be twenty-one, I was astonished at how much he had learned in seven years.

— Mark Twain

*I*n a large house there are articles not only of gold and silver, but also of wood and clay; some are for noble purposes and some for ignoble.

— *2 Timothy 2:20*

FIFTY-FOUR

Danger Never Takes a Vacation

Toddlers tend to love ornate and expensive things. They get their attention. Toddlers know good taste when they see it. They taste, they lick, and they want to touch. They love to hold and examine things. And sometimes things get pulled down on top of them.

For babies the potential risk is falling. They fall from furniture or down stairs. Toddlers are at risk for putting things in their mouths. Medicine resembles candy. Cleaning products may look like sweet beverages. Look around your house daily for things that pose danger. Realize that the interior of your house is constantly changing. We bring things in. We take things out. We buy new things for the house. We decorate differently. But no matter the aesthetic beauty, some things must go or remain in storage. Post the poison control number on your refrigerator: 1-800-222-1222. Then keep a constant watch. Accidents do happen.

> Danger never takes a vacation.
> — Anonymous

𝒜 hot-tempered man must pay the penalty; if you rescue him, you will have to do it again.

— *Proverbs 19:19*

FIFTY-FIVE
Why Your Child Should Suffer the Consequences

As parents, our children will need support, whether it's emotional support, financial support, praise, love, or all of these. But there's a difference between having a need versus being needy. Needy children believe their emotional problems will produce overwhelming sympathy from us. And over time, this sympathy can lead us to becoming their enablers. This produces an unhealthy cycle of bad behavior followed by rescuing. Never respond to your child's bad behavior out of guilt. You'll rescue every time.

Sometimes our children must suffer the consequences of their actions. If you rescue them from every consequence, they will fail to learn the lesson. They know you will always be there to solve their problems and to protect them. Sure, the last thing we want is for our children to suffer. But by suffering the consequences of their actions, it will make them independent thinkers. So show love by allowing consequences. Remember, children want boundaries.

> There is always a moment in childhood
> when the door opens and lets the future in.
> — *Graham Greene*

I belong to my lover, and his desire is for me.

— *Song of Songs 7:10*

FIFTY-SIX
Why a Baby Changes the Chemistry of Your Marriage

What you once were as a couple is no more. The chemistry changes after the baby is born. Your focus on each other is gone. Your child is number one. This is as it should be, but the shift in priorities creates a void in your relationship. This is the reason loyalty becomes an issue with new parents. You will need to know that nothing will ever change between you. Don't let intimacy suffer at the hands of parenthood.

So make a promise to one another. Discuss how the baby has changed the chemistry of your marriage. Then set some dates when you will spend time together as a couple. Don't be a martyr on this one. You don't need to sacrifice your relationship for the sake of the baby. Remain loyal to one another. Maybe go to dinner. Go see a movie. Work on your relationship just as hard as you work on your parenting skills. Great parents love one another first. They make intimacy a factor in their parenting style.

> Communication leads to community, that is,
> to understanding, intimacy and mutual valuing.
> — *Rollo May*

𝒯each me to do your will, for you are my God; may your good Spirit lead me on level ground.

— *Psalm 143:10*

FIFTY-SEVEN
You Must Hate the Word "Must"

*I*t seems as if we spend a lot of time demanding something of our children. We demand they get out of bed and get dressed, that they clean up their toys. But what if you presented your demand as a question?

"Can you pick up your toys?"

"Can you put your coat on?"

Asking them to do something, instead of demanding, gives them an opportunity to make the right choice. Then reward them with praise. This shows them that making the right choice pleases you. And whether you know it or not, every child wants to please the parent above all.

I would much rather say that every time you make a choice you are turning the central part of you, the part that chooses, into something a little different from what it was before.
— C. S. Lewis

*D*ishonest money dwindles away, but he who gathers money little by little makes it grow.

— *Proverbs 13:11*

FIFTY-EIGHT
The Money Crunch

By the second year your baby will have outgrown most of the clothes and toys you received as gifts. If you aren't careful, this void will create a money crunch in the second year. Once your surplus items are all gone, your monthly budget will increase. This is why your baby's first year budget is skewed.

So set your first year budget according to the baby's second year. Do this by adding up the expenditures as if you were starting the first year with no gifts. Add up the cost of diapers, prescriptions, doctor visit co-payments, clothes, and so on. Then live on this second-year budget for the first year. Keep the surplus money in a savings account. This way you will have some emergency money put away for the second year. Plus, it won't be a huge shock when your expenditures increase the second year.

> Money will come to you when you are doing the right thing.
> — *Michael Phillips*

*L*isten, my sons, to a father's instruction; pay attention and gain understanding.

— *Proverbs 4:1*

FIFTY-NINE
How a Father Can Make His Child Listen

One day your child will stand at the door and announce in a shrill voice, "Daddy's home!" It's the grand moment of every day. Never do we get the attention of our children more than we do at this age. Then they grow up and no longer await our arrival. So look forward to this moment. Parents: hug your children. Pick them up. Spin them around. Kiss them. Talk to them as if they are the crown jewel of your day. They will listen. They will smile. So don't let these moments slip away.

When you come home from work, have some type of teaching moment each day—even if it's only for fifteen seconds. Bring home an item from work. Tell them how it's used at your workplace. This teaching opportunity will pass quickly, so seize it. It helps children recognize that their parents possess wisdom. Later in life, they will come to you for advice. It will be automatic.

I felt something impossible for me to explain in words. Then, when they took her away, it hit me. I got scared all over again and began to feel giddy. Then it came to me…I was a father.
— *Nat King Cole*

$\mathcal{S}$he placed the child in [a basket] and put it among the reeds along the bank of the Nile.

— *Exodus 2:3*

SIXTY
Dealing with Separation Anxiety

Moses cried while his basket floated down the Nile. What was he crying about? Was it the fact that he was being separated from his mother? We can't be sure. But our babies can show signs of separation anxiety as early as six months old. The worst stage usually happens between twelve and eighteen months. They sense this separation even before it happens, especially from their mother. Remember, their crying is no real danger. It's phantom fear. But it will pass.

One of the ways to lessen this anxiety is to make your child feel safe at the new location or with the sitter. Warm the atmosphere with love and joy. When the moment comes to say good-bye, say it and leave. Don't linger and come back. It will only make things more difficult. Trust. Moses' mother knew he would be back in her arms, and he was—she was chosen by Pharaoh's daughter to nurse him.

If a child is to keep his inborn sense of wonder, he needs the companionship of at least one adult who can share it, rediscovering with him the joy, excitement and mystery of the world we live in.
— *Rachel Carson*

*T*ruthful lips endure forever, but a lying tongue lasts only a moment.

— *Proverbs 12:19*

SIXTY-ONE
Liar, Liar, Pants on Fire

Children at heart are honest. They want to tell the truth. But sometimes they lie because they fear being punished. They don't know lying will get them in even more trouble. Sometimes children lie because their parents lie. They watch us get out of trouble by lying, so maybe they have learned the craft of lying from us. Who knows? But they experience our white lies when we say we will take them to a ball game and never do. We teach them how to deceive when we answer the phone and lie about someone being home. "She's not here," we say, when she's standing beside us. So watch the white lies you tell and teach your children that lying adds to our problems. Lies never take the trouble away.

> Lying is done with words and also with silence.
> — *Adrienne Rich*

For to see your face is like seeing the face of God.

— *Genesis 33:10*

SIXTY-TWO
Daily Face Time

Frogs never see the face of their mothers. They can only see sudden movements that keep it safe from predators. But humans see much more. We can behold a mother's face. And face time is a sought after commodity. We love to hold our babies and coo into their faces. We adore every twitch. We smile when they smile. But in the beginning, it's hard to tell a gaseous smile from a real one. The faces they make in the first few weeks have very little to do with seeing our faces. But then the day arrives. It gets marked down in our baby journals. We call for others to come and see. Because there will come a day when they will see your face and smile a real smile. They will behold you as you behold them. And it's a glorious day. This is when you feel like a real mother. This will be the connection that will get you through the long nights and the nasty diapers. Your baby smiled!

> To love another person is to see the face of God.
> — *Victor Hugo*

After Jesus had finished instructing his twelve disciples, he went on from there to teach and preach in the towns of Galilee.

— *Matthew 11:1*

SIXTY-THREE
GETTING DADDY IN THE GAME

Even Jesus' disciples needed training. They were crude fishermen—uneducated in saving souls—but willing to help Jesus with the Great Commission. Still, they needed a few tips. So do new fathers.

Is your man squeamish about baby things? Is he reluctant to hold the baby? Is he afraid of what he may do wrong? It could be that he is inexperienced when it comes to babies. Maybe he doesn't know how to help. So vocalize your needs. Make a list of the different duties you need help with. Then discuss the list over dinner. It's easier to talk to a man who's putting food in his mouth.

Start the list with simple tasks. Put the hard ones at the end. Then allow him time to conquer the simple ones first. If he's using his awkwardness as an excuse not to help, then be more direct. Tell him where he's not stepping up. When he makes wonderful progress, praise him. This feedback will boost his confidence. And sometimes confidence is all we need.

> If God can work through me, he can work through anyone.
> — *St. Francis of Assisi*

The wise in heart are called discerning, and pleasant words promote instruction.

— *Proverbs 16:21*

SIXTY-FOUR
The Power of Dr. Seuss's Words

For Dr. Albert Sprinkle

Children love repetition. "Read it again," they say. By the time they make it to kindergarten, we will have their favorite book memorized. We will be sick of Dr. Seuss. We will not like his Green Eggs and Ham. We will grow weary counting One Fish, Two Fish, Red Fish, Blue Fish. We will grow tired of watching people Hop on Pop. This is when moving on will be a delight. But our children will never lean on us and enjoy our presence as much as they will in this moment of their lives. Linger in the reading-to-them stage, and enjoy it. Take a moment each time you read to them, and notice their rapt attention. Watch how peaceful Dr. Seuss's words are to them.

> The more that you read, the more things you will know.
> The more that you learn, the more places you'll go.
> — *Dr. Seuss*

The cheerful heart has a continual feast.

— *Proverbs 15:15*

SIXTY-FIVE
Babies and Their Toys

*T*oddlers are playing best when they explore. They love kitchen cabinets. Doors, too. But watch those little fingers. And you might as well put away all the trinkets. They will grab them and pull them down. All of this is to be expected. So remember the way they play is by exploring. So let them. Give them toys that open their imaginations. Blocks and Legos provide a wealth of curiosity. So will a wooden spoon and a pan. Give them cups at bath time. A bath with many toys is a delight. It's never a chore if you make it fun.

Build three thirty-minute segments of exploring play into their days. Turn off the television. Take away motorized toys and computer games. Make the play creative. It's an important aspect of growth. We live in a world of spectator play, which diminishes our children's imagination. Whatever you do, keep them thinking.

> Creativity is not the finding of a thing, but
> the making something out of it after it is found.
> — *James Russell Lowell*

God heard the boy crying, and the angel of God called to Hagar from heaven and said to her, "What is the matter, Hagar? Do not be afraid; God has heard the boy crying as he lies there."

— *Genesis 21:17*

SIXTY-SIX
How to Fix a Fussy Baby

Genesis 21:17 says, "God heard the boy crying…" You know it's bad when God sends an angel to quiet a child. Fussy babies can get beneath your skin. Sometimes we think the culprit is a wet diaper. But the diaper is dry, and the baby still cries. Once the diaper is ruled out, we believe the baby may be hungry. But he will not eat. So we decide he is sick, so we take him to the doctor. Then the doctor says the terrible word, "Colic."

Colic is the hardest of all our baby's woes. We just don't know how to treat it. Some think a change in the baby's diet may help. Others advise us to be holistic. Others swear by certain songs sung in reverse. So who knows? Maybe pray for an angel. It can get that desperate sometimes. But be of good cheer. Many parents have overcome the colic stage. They persevered. So don't give up. Colic goes as suddenly as it arrives.

> Few things are impossible to diligence and skill.
> Great works are performed not by strength, but perseverance.
> — *Samuel Johnson*

$\mathcal{S}$cream in terror…

— *Isaiah 10:30, NLT*

SIXTY-SEVEN
Screaming Babies

Some babies are screamers and there's no real reason why. Maybe they love the sound of their voices. Maybe they receive a reaction from others. Who knows? But sometimes they enjoy how tense it makes us. It's their sly way of control. And after you make sure nothing is wrong, and the screaming continues, you may have to cling to one reassuring thought, "No one gets two screamers." Of course there's no real validity in this statement, either. But you may have to play a mental trick on yourself. Tell yourself that this too shall pass. Babies aren't screamers for life. There's that transitional moment when the child stops screaming and the parent begins. We scream at the mess they make. We scream at them to be nice, to keep their hands to themselves, to take the garbage out, to get out of bed and go to school, to come home on time. So be patient. You will get your turn to scream.

> Patience is bitter, but its fruit is sweet.
> — *Aristotle*

*T*here is a time for everything, and a season for every activity under heaven.

— *Ecclesiastes 3:1*

SIXTY-EIGHT
Learning to Transition through Growth Stages

*T*ransitions are never easy. About the time we get competent on one level our baby reaches another developmental growth stage, and things change. Their growth spurts are like booster stages of a rocket. One falls away as the other rocket begins. So you must learn to transition with every new development. Diaper changing soon becomes potty training. Nursing becomes spoon-feeding. Crawling becomes walking. Jabbering becomes talking. Riding bicycles becomes driving cars. Childhood is full of transitions. So the key to making easy and smooth transitions is to brainstorm goals for the future. How will the transition from crawling to walking change your current parenting? How will you potty train? Do you have a highchair? Have you decided on what kind of baby food? If you can sit down before a growth transition occurs and brainstorm, then the stress of each transition will be diminished. So be prepared. Stay ahead of every growth spurt.

> He overcomes a stout enemy who overcomes his own anger.
> — *Aristotle*

And this is my prayer: that your love may abound more and more in knowledge and depth of insight.

— *Philippians 1:9*

SIXTY-NINE
How to Pray for Our Children

Prayer works. We know this. But sometimes it feels awkward. We don't know exactly how to pray for our children. In Philippians 1:9, the apostle Paul gives us a great model prayer. He wrote, "This is my prayer for you…" And Paul's emphasis in this prayer is love. He longs to see it abound. He takes prayer to the highest pinnacle and repositions our thoughts on the love of God.

Our children need to see us reaching higher for God. It will increase their depth of insight. So make time to pray for your children. Let them hear you pray. Hold their hands. Speak softly. Be gentle. When a parent participates in prayer with and for their children, it reveals the heart of God to them. So make it a nightly habit. Create a moment of godly inspiration for the both of you.

A satisfying prayer life elevates and purifies every act of body and mind and integrates the entire personality into a single spiritual unit. In the long pull we pray only as well as we live.
— A. W. Tozer

$\mathcal{S}$o Moses thought, "I will go over and see this strange sight—why the bush does not burn up." When the LORD saw that he had gone over to look, God called to him from within the bush, "Moses! Moses!" And Moses said, "Here I am."

— *Exodus 3:3–4*

SEVENTY
Listen for the Whisper of God's Call

*F*inding alone time is difficult after having a baby. There are always duties that call for our attention. The laundry piles up, the house needs cleaning, the dog needs a bath, the bills need to be paid. And it's easy to hear the voices of our duties over the whisper of our Lord. It's always easy to be active and forget about the One who longs to be with us. Moses had to leave his duties and his flock. He had to turn aside and say, "Here I am."

At some point in your day, stop and say to God, "Here I am." This is what the psalmist was doing when he said, "I have stilled and quieted my soul; like a weaned child with its mother, like a weaned child is my soul within me" (Ps 131:2). And if we listen closely, we will hear God say, "Peace, my child." This is the reward of alone time with God.

> Be at peace with your own soul, then
> heaven and earth will be at peace with you.
> — *St. Jerome*

A gentle answer turns away wrath, but a harsh word stirs up anger.

— *Proverbs 15:1*

SEVENTY-ONE
How to Calm an Angry Child

They don't call it the terrible twos for nothing. A child's anger is hard to calm. You can't fight anger with more anger. Yelling never gets the job done, nor does ignoring a temper tantrum. But using a gentle voice soothes wrath. It's like baby powder on a chapped child. A child uses outbursts as a means to control us. If we allow it, we have created a brat. And condoning outbursts is never the best thing for a child.

Anger has its good side, so you never want to break a child's will. But when anger is being used against us as a manipulating tool, then it becomes bad behavior. So first diffuse it with a gentle answer, and then discipline the best you know how.

> Holding on to anger, resentment, and hurt only gives you tense muscles, a headache and a sore jaw from clenching your teeth.
> — *Joan Lunden*

She opened it and saw the baby.

— *Exodus 2:6*

SEVENTY-TWO
There Are No Homely Babies

*Y*our baby will be introduced repeatedly. Everyone will want to see your baby. They look for some kind of resemblance, but in the beginning, our babies usually resemble cone heads or Shrek more than they resemble us. Babies tend to be homely before they are beautiful. So don't be hurt if someone doesn't comment on the beauty of your child. Some people don't know how to give compliments because they are in competition with the rest of the new parents in the world. No doubt you will have friends like this. But never get upset about their reactions to your baby. The only beautiful baby they know lives with them.

Don't place your child before the world with expectations that the world will worship her beauty the way you do. It's not reality. So don't turn every introduction into a beauty pageant. Cherish all of these things inside you the way Mary did with Christ (Luke 2:19). And always remember that homely babies grow up to be beautiful people.

> I am not beautiful. My mother once called me an ugly duckling.
> But, listed separately, I have a few good features.
> — *Audrey Hepburn*

*I*n all the travels of the Israelites, whenever the cloud lifted from above the tabernacle, they would set out.

— *Exodus 40:36*

SEVENTY-THREE
Oh! The Places You Won't Go

*T*he Israelites were always ready to travel. They never knew when God would move them on to a new location. It sounds hectic. They were probably tired because travel will wear you out. So will eating out with a fussy baby. Nobody enjoys the meal. Even going to a nephew's ball game is dictated by weather conditions. No one wants to carry their baby into sweltering heat or a cold night. Even attending church becomes a hassle. It can feel like moving day. But don't stay at home because it would be easier. Travel can be good for you and your baby. Getting out changes the scenery. Babies enjoy new stimuli. Travel makes for great distraction. So you will only need to plan for each trip. Be sure to pack your baby bag with all of the essentials. Make a checklist. Cover the bases. Think ahead about how, when, where your baby will nap or play. Then pack accordingly.

Your life will be no better than the plans you make, and the action you take. You are the architect and builder of your own life, fortune, and destiny.

— *Alfred Montapert*

𝒯hey too lived near relatives in Jerusalem.

— *1 Chronicles 9:38*

SEVENTY-FOUR

State the Obvious for Problematic Relatives

Relatives are a double-edged sword, especially the ones who go against your parenting wishes. Problematic relatives give your child unauthorized sweets. They teach him that hitting is fun. Then they feel chastised if you tell them to stop spoiling your child. You have to love them, but do you have to like their ways? The answer is blowing in the wind, it seems. It depends on how far they live from you. It depends on how much you respect your own parenting style.

Distance can be a good thing, but it's not always the answer. When you can't move away, you must confront them. But for some of us confrontation is difficult. We don't want to seem unloving. But letting your feelings and ideas known will ease your own tension. Problematic relatives will respect your views. So talk. Let them know how you feel. Tell them how their behavior is affecting your parenting skills. This is healthier and cheaper than moving away.

> To confront a person with his own shadow
> is to show him his own light.
> — *Carl Jung*

*Y*our face, LORD, I will seek.

— *Psalm 27:8*

SEVENTY-FIVE
Peek-a-Boo

*B*abies love peek-a-boo. They love the surprise on our faces. So play it often. Engage your child's emotions by showing that Mommy and Daddy have emotions, too. Make a face. Act as if you are crying or laughing. Babies love to imitate our behavior, and they also need this type of interaction with their parents. So buy a toy drum and sit on the floor with them. Lightly play the drum, and then let them have a turn. Show surprise when they make a noise. Behavioral psychology has taught us that such play awakens awareness and creates depth of feeling.

So communicate through your facial expressions. It will help you learn what your baby may be feeling before he or she gets to the verbal stage.

> The essence of pleasure is spontaneity.
> — *Germaine Greer*

*W*hen you lie down, your sleep will be sweet.

— *Proverbs 3:24*

SEVENTY-SIX
Sweet Dreams

Sleeping babies are peaceful to watch. Not a care on their faces, not a single bill on their minds. Just sleep, just rest. They aren't worried they will wake up to a bare cupboard or that the energy bill will be too high to pay. This is why we like watching sleeping babies. Their sleep has a calming effect. But, we need to be aware of the dangers they face while sleeping.

It is our job to control our babies' sleeping environment. So remove loose bedding and stuffed toys from the crib. Put babies on their backs. Don't let them sleep with you. It increases their risk of suffocation. Check on them periodically. Maybe invest in a baby monitor. Getting them to sleep is just the beginning. Keeping them safe while they sleep is the subsequent step. And always tell them, "Sweet dreams." It will soothe both parent and child.

> People who say they sleep like a baby usually don't have one.
> — *Leo J. Burke*

*T*hough my father and mother forsake me, the LORD will receive me.

— *Psalm 27:10*

SEVENTY-SEVEN
The Pain of Divorce

*B*eing married is not easy. The divorce rate is up. Time spent together as a family is down, which is hard on children. Divorce disrupts what they believe is a safe environment. It causes them to feel alone. This is not to say they won't adjust and survive a divorce. They will. Children are resilient. But the wound remains, a wound that will need nurturing to heal.

Some children live in the fear that their parents might split. They watch their friend's parents divorce. It makes them wonder about us. So it is not a bad idea to speak to them about how much you love each other. Knowing you are in love with your spouse creates a shield of comfort around a child. This is why you should show affection toward one another in the presence of your child. It protects them against the fear of separation followed by divorce.

> We do not err because truth is difficult to see.
> It is visible at a glance.
> — *Alexander Solzhenitsyn*

I have heard the grumbling of the Israelites.

— *Exodus 16:12*

SEVENTY-EIGHT
Stop That Whining!

A grumbling adult or a whining child is like fingernails on a chalkboard. Whining grates on everyone's nerves. So how do you stop the whining?

Putting an end to whining requires lots of patience. Children whine as a means of communication. It says they are frustrated, or unhappy, or hurting. Tell them you understand they are upset, but that whining will not make things better. If they can communicate to you in a normal voice, you will listen to them and try to help them solve their problem. When faced with whining, empathy—not anger—is the answer.

> Realize that if you have time to whine and complain about something, then you have the time to do something about it.
>
> — *Anthony J. D'Angelo*

How happy I am! The women will call me happy.

— Genesis 30:13

SEVENTY-NINE
How to Get Happy

*H*appiness isn't all the money in the world. It's not beauty or fame. It's not power. Happiness is a state of mind, even when we aren't happy about our circumstances. The apostle Paul believed our thoughts dictate our contentment. He wrote, "If anything is excellent or praiseworthy—think about such things" (Phil 4:8). So what we think matters.

If you can think yourself into a funk, then you can think yourself out of it. Paul went on to say, "I have learned to be content whatever the circumstances" (Phil 4:11). He had learned contentment in every aspect of life. He said it's all in the One you trust. He never focused on his current circumstances. He believed what St. Francis of Assisi said later, "While you are proclaiming peace with your lips, be careful to have it even more fully in your heart." So cultivate happiness by thinking excellent and praiseworthy thoughts.

Do not measure your loss by itself; if you do, it will seem intolerable; but if you will take all human affairs into account you will find that some comfort is to be derived from them.

— *St. Basil*

$\mathcal{T}$hen you will understand what is right and just and fair—every good path.

— *Proverbs 2:9*

EIGHTY

Being Fair to Grandparents

Everyone will want time with the new baby. Grandparents are no exception. Grandparents on both sides of the family will want equal time, and this is a good thing. Grandparents have been hoping for this baby since your wedding day. Sure, they may seem fanatical about spending time with the baby, but this is where you need to see their good intentions. Their actions may be interpreted as overbearing when in actuality it may be joy. So be fair while remaining sensitive to both sides. Draw boundaries early on. Make them flexible, yet firm. It sounds heartless, but you'll be happy you did it. It makes it less personal for you. Withholding your baby from the grandparents because you think they are trying to control you is being extreme in the opposite direction. Balance is the key. And it's always better to err on the side of what brings joy to others.

What children need most are the essentials that grandparents provide in abundance. They give unconditional love, kindness, patience, humor, comfort, lessons in life. And, most importantly, cookies.
— *Rudolph Giuliani*

*T*he wolf will live with the lamb, the leopard will lie down with the goat, the calf and the lion and the yearling together; and a little child will lead them.

— *Isaiah 11:6*

EIGHTY-ONE
Pets and Babies

$\mathcal{P}$ets and babies are a concern. No one knows how your pet will respond to your baby. In the beginning, your pet may become jealous or just be curious. So allow this curiosity with heightened concern. Be prepared, but remain calm. Don't give baby or pet a reason to be alarmed. Pets can usually sense your nervousness as fear.

If you think there may be a conflict with your pet, you may need to remove the pet from your home. This will be a shock to the pet, but usually pets adapt to a new environment. On the other hand, if pet and baby have no conflict, then you shouldn't rearrange the living quarters. Still, remain on the cautious side. You can never be too safe. But most of the time pets and babies make great friends. They welcome the new relationship.

It is almost impossible for one to be cruel to animals and kind to humans. If children are permitted to be cruel to their pets and other animals, they easily learn to get the same pleasure from the misery of fellow-humans. Such tendencies can easily lead to crime.
— *Fred A. McGrand*

I myself will guarantee his safety.

— *Genesis 43:9*

EIGHTY-TWO
From the Crib to the Bed

*A*ll children eventually climb out of the crib. They go beyond the confinements they never questioned as babies. At this moment a child-development crisis hits—they are too big for a crib, but they seem too small for a bed. So the best move is forward. Introduce them to their new bed. Make it a positive experience. Tell them they are a big girl or big boy now. Maybe buy new sheets featuring their favorite television character. Then put rails on their new bed for safety. If they climb out of bed, lead them back. Continue with a minimum of verbal communication—until they remain in bed. Be diligent.

The point is to develop the childlike inclination for play and the childlike desire for recognition and to guide the child over to important fields for society.
— *Albert Einstein*

And you must show mercy to those whose faith is wavering.

— *Jude 1:22, NLT*

EIGHTY-THREE
Reach Back Once You Get There

One of the most rewarding aspects of being a parent is being able to encourage other parents. All of us have our doubts when we first start out. But soon we get beyond them with the right help. So try to reach out to new parents in your church, in your neighborhood, or in your extended family. Someone needs you. They need a sounding board. All of us wish we had someone to silence our doubts, to tell us that our thinking is faulty, to tell us it is normal to doubt our ability at times. So reach back. Help others. Today, in hospitals all over America, babies are being placed into the arms of doubting parents. They are fearful of not doing the right things— you remember. Mother Teresa said, "Be a living expression of God's kindness." You can make a difference. Be creative. Set aside time each week for others. Maybe start a book club around parenting. But don't preach. Just love them. Quiet their fears. Be there. Show mercy.

> I would rather make mistakes in kindness and compassion
> than work miracles in unkindness and hardness.
> — *Mother Teresa*

Then he went down and talked with the woman, and he liked her.

— Judges 14:7

EIGHTY-FOUR
Remember the Romance

*T*alking about love, thinking about love, and being loved can mean different things to different people. Only you know what to talk about when you talk about love. But, without communication, love can become an idea. It can become a feeling we once felt. So never focus all of your love on the baby. Remember, love brought you together, not a baby. And sometimes you will need to cultivate love once again. For love gets choked out when we do more worrying than loving. So quiet your soul when you talk about love. Don't think about the bills, about what might happen to your baby in the future, about how household chores aren't done. Instead, think about what you said on your wedding day. Think about the love you felt on that day, and then talk about it. Thinking about love can rekindle it. It can make you like one another again.

Loving someone is not about keeping things from them, or protecting them or controlling what they feel, it's about letting them be free.

— A.W. Cass

[*B*enaiah] also went down into a pit on a snowy day and killed a lion.

— *2 Samuel 23:20*

EIGHTY-FIVE
How to Get out of the Pits

*B*enaiah was walking along on a snowy day and fell into a lion's pit. And if that wasn't bad enough, a lion was occupying the pit. You talk about having a bad day!

Life has a way of dropping us into an occupied lion's pit. Sometimes fights are chosen for us. Like Benaiah, we must face the lion in the pit and fight. We can't defeat something we are unwilling to face. So first accept your situation, then fight, claw, gouge, scramble—do whatever it takes to defeat the lion. Maybe your lion is doubt. Maybe it's an outrageous bill. Maybe it's a birth defect. Maybe it's a bad marriage. Whatever your lion may be, you must first decide to fight. If Benaiah had succumbed to fear, it would have meant lunch for the lion. So find the courage it takes to defeat your lion. Then fight!

Life is not easy for any of us. But what of that? We must have perseverance and above all confidence in ourselves. We must believe that we are gifted for something and that this thing must be attained.
— *Marie Curie*

*I*mpress them on your children. Talk about them when you sit at home and when you walk along the road, when you lie down and when you get up.

— *Deuteronomy 6:7*

EIGHTY-SIX
What You Should Be Talking About

*T*oo much talk about God becomes convoluted droning, and our children stop listening. But Moses believed that our children never grow weary of hearing about God. Usually, you can start teaching them when they turn two. And remember that it's all in the way we present it. Never force God on them. Always lead, guide, and direct them to God's heart.

Watch for teachable moments when you can demonstrate the love of God toward other people. Talk about honesty with your children. Teach about dignity. Show them how to pray. Read to them. Make faith part of their nighttime routine. A book in bed, then good-night prayers. It's our Christian duty as a parent. Plus, our children are learning from watching our actions. So walk out your faith before your children. You may even want to put a few scripture verses on the refrigerator. Keep God ever present.

As each new generation begins, another moves aside to make room.
Life seems so short; that's why every moment counts.
— *Sue Stern*

Only a fool despises a parent's discipline; whoever learns from correction is wise.

— *Proverbs 15:5, NLT*

EIGHTY-SEVEN
A Unified Front

*D*on't teach your child how to play both sides to the middle. If Mommy says no then Daddy should support her and vice versa. Make an agreement with your spouse. If one says no, then don't allow your child to run to the other one for a reversal. A unified front conquers a double-minded parenting style. This means that you may not agree on some parenting issues, but you must support each other's decision when you tell your child yes or no. If you disagree on the subject, talk about it later in private. Never disagree in front of your child. This only teaches him how to work the two of you. And children learn quickly who the easy parent is, and they will always plead their case in a winsome tone. It's their little work behind the scenes. So keep a unified front. Respect your spouse.

> After observing the loved and the unloved,
> we found the loved ones rarely tried to manipulate others.
> — *W. W. Broadbent*

And nd the LORD directed me at that time to teach.

— *Deuteronomy 4:14*

EIGHTY-EIGHT
Potty Time

Getting through the potty stage can be trying for parents and children alike. It takes patience and some ingenuity. So do it in stages. Invest in a portable potty for children. Put it in the bathroom for a few weeks before you actually have them use it. Talk to them about it. Make it sound like an infomercial. Sell it night and day. Offer rewards. Anything goes. Try a few videos. But remember that it will take a few failed attempts. Switching from diapers to underwear may mean a few accidents. Expect this. But never force them before they are ready. Let it come to them naturally. Frustration never helps. Go at their rate. That's the key.

> Patience is the companion of wisdom.
> — St. Augustine

*B*ut don't begin until you count the cost. For who would begin construction of a building without first calculating the cost to see if there is enough money to finish it?

— *Luke 14:28, NLT*

EIGHTY-NINE

Renew Your Commitment as a Parent Each Day

*J*esus was a carpenter before he was our Messiah. He knew how to cut wood. He built a few things in his lifetime. He started early in the morning, rising before daylight. He went to the woodshop and created. He knew how to swing a hammer. He knew how to estimate a job. He could count the cost before he built his furniture. And every day when you rise to be a loving parent, remind yourself of the cost involved. Parenting is a daily commitment to work for the welfare of your child. Renew it each morning. Tell yourself there's no hill too steep to climb, no valley too deep to cross when it comes to raising your children. Think of their future. This is what you're fulfilling for them. You are making a way, their way. You're helping them mature. And the cost may be great, but your love is greater. Think of our Lord. His love for us was greater than the cost of the Cross.

Let nothing disturb thee; / Let nothing dismay thee; / All thing pass; / God never changes. / Patience attains / All that it strives for. / He who has God / Finds he lacks nothing: / God alone suffices.
— *St. Teresa of Avila*

*Y*ou want something but don't get it. You kill and covet, but you cannot have what you want. You quarrel and fight. You do not have, because you do not ask God.

— *James 4:2*

NINETY
Armchair Husbands

Sometimes husbands fail to see the chores and never lift a finger to help. This could be a communication breakdown. Sure, he should be able to see that you need help. But some men can't or won't, so be verbal without being accusatory. Use language that disarms his defenses. And only you will know the key to this secret, only you will know what works and what has failed to work in the past. Some men respond to lists. Other men take action when asked. So ask, as the Bible says, "You do not have because you do not ask...." (Jas 4:2). Now James didn't have a husband in mind when he wrote this. The idea is to include God as a partner in your faith. And sometimes mothers fail to see fathers as partners in parenting. The one thing every husband will respond to is the baby. So let him help. Share responsibilities. Trust him. Give him baby-related tasks. Then throw in a few peripheral chores such as taking out the trash.

> Light is the task when many share the toil.
> — *Homer*

We do not dare to classify or compare ourselves with some who commend themselves. When they measure themselves by themselves and compare themselves with themselves, they are not wise.

— *2 Corinthians 10:12*

Ninety-One
Friends Don't Let Friends Compete

One of the rude awakenings of parenting is how everyone may not generally share excitement for your child's milestones. Sometimes jealousy runs deep between mothers. Competition is in our blood. And some mothers will one-up you every time you share milestones with them. Either their child accomplished that stage when he was two weeks old, or he skipped that step to move on to the next one. So acknowledge this for what it is—competition. It's nothing more than playground talk. Do you remember when you told a friend that your father could beat up their father? It seems ridiculous now. But comparison carried so much weight back then.

When you sense that you are in competition with another mother, don't share milestones. You will end up avoiding each other in the end because there's no way to gauge a clear winner. Just as your father never dueled with someone else's father on the playground, don't get involved in this pure drivel.

> Comparisons do ofttime great grievance.
> — *John Lydgate*

One day Jesus was praying in a certain place. When he finished, one of his disciples said to him, "Lord, teach us to pray."

— *Luke 11:1*

NINETY-TWO
Why You Should Pray with Your Spouse

Maybe you are lying in bed beside your spouse reading this book. Maybe you are drinking coffee together and starting your morning with a devotional. This is good. Try to build into your marriage a time when you pray together or read a devotional together. Making contact with your spouse soul-to-soul deepens love. It makes love more than an emotion. Every time you pray together it creates a bond that allows love to always protect, always trust, always hope, always persevere (1 Cor 13:7). It's the one thing Jesus' disciples asked him to teach them. "Teach us to pray," they said. Something happened to them when Jesus prayed, something larger than "teach us to work miracles," or "teach us to preach." They sensed Jesus' love when he prayed. This is why praying with your spouse is important. They will sense your love and affection for them. They will feel protected by this love, and at the end of a long and tiring day of parenting, love may be all you need.

> He prayeth well who loveth well.
> — *Samuel Taylor Coleridge*

$\mathcal{B}$e strong and courageous.

— *Deuteronomy 31:6*

NINETY-THREE
How to Choose the Right Day Care

Mentioning day care can send horror through a parent's heart. We want to stay at home with our baby. We worry our baby will be neglected. "Who is holding my baby?" "Is anyone holding my baby?" These questions can play in the back of your mind during the workday. It's tough. Sure, every mother should be her own day care. But this is unrealistic. These days, most mothers work outside the home. So day care is the only option when relatives aren't near and available. You will have to trust your instincts when it comes to choosing a day care. Investigate. Make sure the day care is accredited. Watch for inconsistencies. Is the staff constantly changing? Do you feel at ease when you walk in the center, or do you sense tension? Only you can know. But don't seek perfection. It's not out there. Leaving your child at day care is hard, but it does get easier. You will eventually be at peace with it.

Peace is a daily, a weekly, a monthly process, gradually changing opinions, slowly eroding old barriers, quietly building new structures.
— *John Fitzgerald Kennedy*

There are "friends" who destroy each other, but a real friend sticks closer than a brother.

— *Proverbs 18:24, NLT*

NINETY-FOUR

Teaching Your Child How to Make Friends

You have to be a friend to have friends. But what do you do when you first start out? You have never had a friend, you have never been a friend—this is your child's dilemma. So keep this in mind. Children do not know how friends should treat each other. They don't know how to introduce themselves if they are shy. So you will have to be the initiator. Get the ball rolling. Go to the park. Call a friend who has a child and set up a playdate. Sharing toys is always a good icebreaker for children. It helps build social skills. Some children advance more quickly than others. Be patient. Just because you are a social butterfly doesn't mean your child should be a social caterpillar. Sometimes our children's personalities are opposite of our own. This is okay. Don't push too hard. Let friendships happen naturally.

> If a man does not make new acquaintances as he advances through life, he will soon find himself left alone.
> — *Samuel Johnson*

Give us nothing but vegetables to eat and water to drink.

— *Daniel 1:12*

NINETY-FIVE
Picky Eaters

*D*aniel was a picky eater. He refused royal food and vied for vegetables and water. Sure, he put himself on this diet. But most toddlers who are picky eaters aren't as food savvy as Daniel. The one thing you don't want to do, though, is become the king and force-feed your child. If your child is growing and looks healthy, then don't be concerned. If her health is seemingly diminishing, then go see your pediatrician.

The one thing you can do is provide a variety of foods at meal and snack times. Let your child choose. But if she doesn't like anything you provide, then move on and wait until the next meal or snack time. Don't fight about it. Get creative. Hide vegetables inside a casserole. Offer vegetable sticks and dressing. Toddlers love to dunk their food. Try yogurt. But if your child wants only junk food, then you should stop offering it. Be aware of manipulation.

> The bearing and the training of a child
> Is woman's wisdom.
> — *Lord Alfred Tennyson*

Patience is better than pride.

— Ecclesiastes 7:8

NINETY-SIX
The Hidden Controller

*P*atience is a parent's virtue, but impatience is what happens when we feel we are losing control. Most of the time our impatience is a control issue. We want our children to abide by our timetable. We want them to do things now! We want them to progress through their stages of growth at our pace. It would bring us so much pride. But this rarely happens. So the next time you become impatient ask yourself if it's a control issue. If it is, then change what you can or realize what you can't change. Our children's growth doesn't respond to our commands.

Hidden emotions that are trying to emerge can make us feel impatient at times. Sometimes we can displace our inner struggles onto our children. It's like kicking the dog at the end of the workday because the boss yelled at us. We can take things out on our children. Be careful here.

> And I must bear What is ordained with patience.
> — *Elizabeth Barrett Browning*

I am telling you now before it happens, so that when it does happen you will believe.

— John 13:19

NINETY-SEVEN
BEFORE AND AFTER SNAPSHOTS

*E*very mother's life consists of before and after snapshots—before the baby was born, before I quit my job, before I put her in day care, before she stopped wearing diapers, before she crawled, before she walked, before she talked. Every moment of a mother's life is like a home improvement show on HGTV. There are before major renovation shots and after shots. Things look and feel so differently. And the good thing about motherhood is how everyday your child is improving and changing, doing things differently. It's so exciting. It's like being on an adventure. And you must see motherhood like this. You are on the greatest adventure of your life. So slow down and enjoy it. Get a lot of before and after shots. You will need them when you start scrapbooking. Plus, the changes seem to happen so suddenly that you will miss them if you are always full of doubt and worry.

> What lies behind us and what lies before us
> are tiny matters compared to what lies within us.
> — *Samuel Taylor Coleridge*

𝓛isten, my son, to your father's instruction and do not forsake your mother's teaching.

— *Proverbs 1:8*

NINETY-EIGHT
Mothers Teach Their Children How to Treat Them

A teacher gave her second-grade students a lesson on science. She explained about magnets and showed how they pick up nails and other bits of iron. Now it was question time and she asked, "My name begins with the letter 'M' and I pick up things. What am I?"

A little boy in the front row answered, "You're a mother."

You will have days when you feel like a magnet instead of a mother. You will feel used, as if everyone expects you to go around and pick up after them. So teaching our children early on that they must pick up after themselves and clean their rooms is imperative. If not, you will raise children like the little boy in second grade who believes his mother is like a magnet. Mothers teach their children how to treat them. So don't teach your children that you are a magnet.

The hand that rocks the cradle is the hand that rules the world.
— *W. S. Ross*

For if God did not spare angels when they sinned, but sent them to hell, putting them into gloomy dungeons to be held for judgment.

— *2 Peter 2:4*

NINETY-NINE
We Can Love Them Too Much

God gave the angels one strike, and they were out. No second chances for angels. This is why scripture says angels marvel at God's leniency with humans (1 Pet 1:12). God seems to have a weakness when it comes to his children and their sins. So will you. It's tempting to let our children get away with murder. We can love them too much when we fail to punish them. An undisciplined child is a brat. Children learn fast when it comes to our discipline. They know how far we'll go before we break. So they push us to the brink, and we can give in too easily and let them off with a warning. Warnings are good, but warnings without follow-through are only empty threats. So warn once. Tell them there will be consequences next time. Then carry out the punishment the next time it occurs.

> The character and history of each child may be a new and poetic experience to the parent, if he will let it.
> — *Margaret Fuller*

*A*nts are creatures of little strength, yet they store up their food in the summer.

— *Proverbs 30:25*

ONE HUNDRED
THE WINTER OF OUR PARENTHOOD

*A*nts love picnics. They march to them in succession. With their tiny feet kicking up like an army of well-trained soldiers on display. They're after the crumbs. They know winter is coming. They know they will have to store their food in summer, so they can eat in winter. But as humans we are only thinking about the picnic. We're not thinking of blustery days. We're in the sun of immediate joy. But let us stop and observe the ants. Let us learn from them.

The first stage of parenthood focuses on the immediate, such as diapers, helping our children learn to speak or walk—much like a picnic. But winter is coming in your parenthood. The empty nest is on its way. So take a chapter from the ant's life—plan for your child's future. Finding financial means to fund college can be difficult in the winter of parenthood. Be prepared.

> None preaches better than the ant, and she says nothing.
> — *Benjamin Franklin*

ABOUT THE AUTHOR

Robert Stofel served as pastor of two churches in Decatur, Alabama. He spent three years in the inner city of Nashville counselling crack addicts and has spoken to thousands across the southern United States. He holds a BS in psychology and did post-graduate work at Gordon-Conwell Theological Seminary. This is his fifth book and the third book in the *Survival Note Series*. He lives in Alabama with his wife, Jill. They have two daughters.